SOUL *Care*

The Lenten Model

Carolyn J. Sweers

By

CAROLYN J. SWEERS

Ordering Information:
For orders and inquiries, please contact:
1-888-375-9818
www.toplinkpublishing.com
bookorder@toplinkpublishing.com

Printed in the United States of America

CONTENTS

Preface

This book began in Lent as a way
to continue my own engagement with the season.

I am by temperament and training a philosopher.
My life and work have been shaped by
moments of mystic communion
which can't be adequately described or named
and is, I presume,
what is pointed to by the word "God".

I have, wherever possible, used a word other than "God"
to refer to the framing Mystery of our lives....
the horizon that draws us toward reverence,
humility
and compassion.

Though I sparingly use the word "God",
it is my hope that persons who speak of God
may recognize some similarities
between what is written here
and what they say
they believe.

The challenge I posed for myself
was to try to describe the Lenten practices
in the way I have experienced them;
a way I hope will be useful for any spiritual seeker
as well as not opposed to Christianity
for those who actively participate in that tradition.

To that end,
I have attempted to explore ways in which
Lent, a season in the Christian year,
has universal applications for human life and development.
This book attempts to enunciate ways in which the season itself,
with its impetus,
its dynamics,
its practices,
has a significance,
a usefulness
that is more universal
than that
of any single
religious tradition.

The primary purpose of this book is to evoke...
not to explain.
To get the most value from this book,
there must be engagement,
dialogue with
and reflection on
one's own experiences
as well as on the spiritual truths
found in the world's religions.

The most important words on the pages that follow
may be the ones you, the reader, write in the margins...
the evoked responses to the printed words.

Spend time with the pages that engage you.
Let the rest go.

LENT
As Spiritual Journey

A Lenten-type season
provides the opportunity
and incentive
for concentrated,
intentional,
mindful
spiritual work,
such as discerning the difference
between appearance ("worldly" values)
and reality (spiritual truths).

The season is rich in transformational potential:
a time to find and live who we *really* are;
a time to ask, "What do we *really* want to do and be?
What do we value most?
Why *do* we so often seek things that neither last nor satisfy?
Why do we so often fail to acknowledge ourselves as spiritual
beings,
linked together...
in community.

The focus of spiritual life is on the eternal,
with what can't be seen,
with what is, in fact, a reversal of the worldly order of things.

Instead of indulging, do without.
Instead of earning and spending and hoarding,
give money to those in need.

Instead of relying on yourself,
pray
or in some way be mindful of the sacred,
in whatever forms
it may appear.

In all three Lenten practices,
priority is given to what is often neglected,
which is to say
the spiritual way that leads to the most fulfilling,
satisfying
way of being—
the life for which we long.

A Lenten type season reminds us
of our true
but often forgotten nature.
It is a time for recognizing
and responding to
our divine origin and destiny.

A Lenten season draws us toward
and into
communion with truths that are eternal
in whatever embodied form they come to us…
in words of scriptures,
poems,
paintings,
relationships
inspirations of various kinds.
These are reminders.
They evoke recollection.
They can enkindle, awaken, activate
our true ,divine-tending, potential.
"This is who you can be," they say.
"This is who you *really* are."

This is the vision that resonates,
that summons,
that compels.

The three Lenten practices:
prayer,
fasting,
almsgiving—
are intimately interconnected.

It is in prayer, or meditative quiet,
that we begin to discern what is of ultimate importance.
It is in prayer (or its equivalent) that we acknowledge
and let ourselves be shaped
by the "framing Mystery" that surrounds our lives.
It is in prayer (or its equivalent)
that we discern what must be given up,
as well as what we need to give.

To Fast is to recognize and intentionally refrain from
attitudes and actions that impose limits on spiritual development
such as selfish grasping,
giving in to irritation and anger,
restlessly seeking diversions,
to name a few.
Lent is reflection time—
time to notice and begin to change
habits and practices
that prevent us from living
the life we *really* want.
Lent is a time to refrain from
mindless living.
Lent is a time
to not let unexamined wants
direct our actions.
Through fasting practices,
one can learn how to give up the lesser for the sake of the greater.
This opens the heart to others and their needs.

Alms are given.
Hearts (and pocketbooks)
respond to
the needs
of others.

There is an essential inwardness to the "Lenten season",
however and whenever it is practiced.
There is inner work to be done
work to find out what is *really* going on with (in) us.

There is inner work to be done
in order to be compassionate.

There is inner work to be done to benefit others
as well as oneself.

What sort of work is that?
How does one do it?

To change our lives, we have to change our minds.
To change our life, we have to change our understanding
of who we are
and what is most important.

We have to train the mind,
reconstruct mental habits
and propensities,
the whole desiring/wanting tendency.

How does one do this?

There is no single answer.
though all of the major world religions provide
contemplative guides and introspective practices.

Each person must seek and find
the method that works best.

It was from Buddhism
that I came to understand the importance of mind training.

It is not external things that harm (or help) us
but the inward effects of them,
a point Jesus made more than once.

Every thought and action has consequences.
Thought patterns (and the actions that stem from them)
resist being changed
even though repetition does not bring satisfaction
and may even cause suffering
to others as well as oneself.

Even when circumstances change,
old patterns tend to be repeated
even when the attempt to impose them on the changed situation
requires more and more energy
and yet is rarely successful
because the old patterns are not appropriate
to/for the changed situation.
There is inertia involved and a strong self-protective aspect
even though that stems from
what spiritual traditions identify as a "false" self.

To find the *true* self
involves (requires) the insight and guidance of
a spiritual tradition.

**Most spiritual traditions stress the importance of
solitude and silence.**

In solitude, we can begin to wean our mind,
our attention,
away from the world
and our usual preoccupations.
Our energy, which is usually directed outward,
reverses course, for a while.
The less important begins to fall away.
In its place begins to arise
something so precious
that one wants nothing else.

Just being physically alone is not enough.
There must be an inner stillness,
a letting go of mental attachments and fixations.
For this, meditation practices can be helpful.

Silence is important.
In silence, we become receptive
to the openings to the Transcendent,
the infinite,
the Divine.
In silence, we experience the "emptiness"
of which spiritual masters speak:
the "emptiness" that is receptivity to
that which arrests our going here and there…
planning, plotting, gaining, regretting, and so forth.

Be still…and know:
the Great Silence
that beckons and blesses.

The self-examination
that is so essential to a Lent like season,
is evoked by a *vision*.

Only an awareness of the Fullness,
the Mystery,
the Divine
can give spiritual practices their purpose,
their richness
and, yes, their joy.

We are, all the time, being addressed by Mystery—
a Mystery that seems connected to
(and probably is)
the deepest center of our own being.

What abides
is not our little anxious self
with its treasures, hopes and commitments.

What abides is something infinitely more expansive.
What abides is the vast and intricate wonder of it all
and the privilege of being here—
being aware.

EvenIf one does not believe in the importance of what is written here, it might be useful to experiment for a period;
acting "as if"
the insights were true…
and seeing what happens.

Be experimental!

Keep track of what works
as you gradually become aware
of the "advantages" of the spiritual life—
the "advantages" of becoming purer in heart,
more generous,
more reverent,
more compassionate.

The process is gradual.
It takes time.
There will be setbacks.
There will be periods in which nothing seems to be happening.

Persevere.

Trust the process!

ASH WEDNESDAY
And The Remembrance
Of Death

Ash Wednesday
(or its equivalent for those who do not keep Lent in traditional
ways
but who want to benefit
from the lessons of the season)
brings the stark reminder
that we, are each of us,
going to die.

On Ash Wednesday, the bracing realism of the day means
that we can no longer evade,
hide,
cover over,
explain away
the fact that we will die.
The day will come
when we will draw our final breath;
our heart will stop;
our body will get cold and stiff.
That's our destination, our destiny.

What is remembered
on Ash Wednesday
is not just death
in the sense of our last breath
but all the limits and losses
that are part of being human.
Should we curse the darkness?
Shall we furiously spend our days
on projects
that screen out
the thought of dying?
Or should we let
the remembrance of death,
our death,
be a summons—
a call to a sacred task?

We will suffer; we will die.
We will lose what we try to grip.
We can't get free from what we try so hard to avoid.
So why is remembering that so important?
Because it is a stark reminder
that we do not have forever
to focus on
what is most important.
And that,
paradoxically,
is good and needed news.

It is because we will die
that the Lenten practices
are so vital.
It is because we will die
that we need to fast,
to pray,
to give alms.

It is because we will die
that we need to look inward;
that we have to be honest about how we live
and what we value;
to give up the lesser
for the sake of the greater.

It is because we will die
that we can and must
be openhearted,
compassionate;
forgiving of the neighbor
and the stranger.

It is because we will die
that we must pray,
must live toward,
and within,
that which abides.

The seeming paradox of Ash Wednesday,
and of the Lenten season itself,
is that the realization,
the awareness of loss,
can be a great gain.
The fact that we will die
is in a way
good news
because it wakes us up
to how short the time,
how urgent the task
of recognizing the spiritual responsibilities
that come from
being human.

The promise of Lent is
that by embracing what is usually avoided (death),
we set our faces toward a radiance
that is beyond all loss or death.

What abides is not our little anxious self
with its treasures,
hopes
and commitments.

What abides is something infinitely more expansive.

What abides is the vast and intricate *wonder* of it all.
And the privilege, though brief,
of being here
and being aware.

FASTING:
Recognizing and Removing
Impediments to Spiritual Growth

Lent is a concentrated period of soul care.
Therefore, it is important to know the conditions of soul growth,
as the masters of the spiritual life have described them.
In addition to the vision of the possibilities,
all agree that some sort of inner "house cleaning" is needed.
This is the task of the various fasting practices.

Fasting is a giving up
but in response to something higher,
better.

Growth requires renunciation.
It is like the life force within a seed.
The husks of the old have to be broken up,
shed,
let go.

The giving up,
the fasting,
is prompted from inside;
made necessary
by the requirements of the soul for its own growth.
It was Huston Smith's description of renunciation in Hinduism
that first brought this point
to my attention.

The task,
the challenge,
is to discern signs of new growth and nurture them.
In that way,
we gradually become
more truly
who we *really* are.

In the traditional Lenten practices,
fasting has to do with food:
giving up certain foods "for Lent";
not eating meat on Fridays, for example.

Though the *fasting* that spiritual growth requires
is more comprehensive than the practices involving food,
food fasting is
a good place to begin.

Not only is food essential to life,
it has powerful emotional associations, too.
Childhood memories.
"Comfort" foods.
Meals used to observe/celebrate special occasions.

How basic is food to our sense of self.
What we eat,
when,
with whom.

It is important to learn to eat *mindfully*:
to not just eat on impulse,
or eat what's near
or what others are consuming.

It is important to pause,
for a moment,
before eating
to recognize our sense of need,
our dependence on food and on those who supply it,
the interconnectedness of human effort and the natural elements.
In the Lenten Practices,
this awareness leads to **alms giving**.

To intentionally change an eating habit or food preference
can bring us face to face with truths about ourselves
we might have preferred to ignore.

The Buddha said that the cause of much human suffering
is desire,
hunger,
craving.
Humans, he said, tend to crave things which don't (can't)
bring satisfaction.
Jesus agreed.

Fasting practices can uncover deep hungers
which can prompt a prayer:
"Give us this day our daily bread."
Give us what we *really* need.

To hunger…is to need to receive.
That is why there is an important link
between prayer and/or meditation
and fasting practices.

One has to discover what one needs for spiritual growth,
and that can be discerned in prayer
and/or meditation.
Without such discernment,
the giving up we do can become
a disguised,
not always thinly,
manifestation of a willfulness
that strengthens the very ego-centered habits
that need to be overcome
or transformed.

An important element in food fasting practices
is to be hungry enough to be reminded
of those who do not have enough to eat
and expressing, at least symbolically,
a connection to them.
That is why fasting is such an important spiritual practice,
and why it is one of the Five Pillars of Islam.

Thus, the Lenten practices of food fasting,
and the desire to give alms,
are linked—
inseparably.

Though there is a very important,
elemental,
food aspect to Lenten fasting,
the fasting practices required by the spiritual life
are far more extensive than this:
the call to fast from the dominance of ego
and self-interest.

Fasting from what does not truly satisfy.
Giving priority to important things that are often neglected.

Fasting from the food that perishes.
Fasting from what does not last.

Giving priority to what is often neglected
as a way toward the most fulfilling,
satisfying way of being—
the sort of life
for which we long.

Essential to all fasting practices
is an awareness of **desire**:
how it works,
how pervasive it is,
and how it tends to increase suffering.
There is, perhaps, a no more perceptive account of this
than the one Buddha gave
in his Four Noble Truths.

Desires arise out of an awareness that something is missing—
something that we think we need.
Desires motivate actions.
We go toward the desired object.
We channel energy toward it.
The desired object, especially if the desire is strong,
tends to dominate awareness.

One desires what one wants but does not have.
There is a tendency to think
that if one has what is desired,
satisfaction will result.
However, as reflection on experience shows,
when the desired object is obtained/attained,
a new desire arises in its place.
Desires seem insatiable.

Desires tend to be sense based…directed outward.

There are several problems with this, spiritually speaking:

1) The outward focus of most desires
has a tendency to create traps and snares.
For we cannot *control* what is external to us.
We cannot hold onto what is always changing.

2) Following desires leads to a distracted mind.
A person in such a state is never satisfied.
He/she has thoughts that keep darting from one thing to another
with the result that the desired objects,
even when attained,
do not bring lasting satisfactions.

3) Desires, once they arise,
tend to have a momentum of their own which,
if left unchecked,
propel one toward the desired object
but not always in positive ways.
Pursuing desires,
without regard for consequences,
tends to cause harm.

4) When desires are frustrated,
mental turbulence is the result
and this turbulence works against the process
of gaining genuine insight—wisdom.
For the latter, introspection,
and quieting of the mind are needed.
But that is not easy to do.

Desire for fulfillment via objects,
persons,
circumstances
is actually a trap.
This is true for all desires, the spiritual masters say,
except the desire that is
"hungering and thirsting for righteousness" (Jesus);
and the desire to be free
of the mind-produced causes of suffering. (Buddha).

When it comes to desires,
reflection/discernment is needed.
We tend to overestimate the attractiveness of the desired object
and we forget the lessons of our own experience
that would show how frequently
getting a desired object
did not result
in lasting satisfaction.

When desires are observed in meditation, or in prayer,
we can notice them as they arise,
and how they gradually diminish when not attended to,
or, at least, not allowed to generate a story—
a string of associations
that keep us wanting what, in fact,
can't satisfy.

Are there states of mind free from selfish desire?
Yes, the calm, contemplative state
in which there is nothing more to want.
A calm, receptive inner place:
Open hearted.
Compassionate.
To get there
there is much fasting
that needs doing.

Inspired by Buddhist meditation experiences,
I have come to recognize
that there is a *mental fasting*
that is important.
It is important to become aware (mindfully)
of the attitudes and actions
that impede,
spiritual development.
It is important to learn how to minimize
or give up
the allures and false promises
that tend to snare us.

The result will be
a gracious,
welcoming openness
to the world
and its people.

WHAT KINDS OF FASTING PRACTICES PROMOTE A SPIRITUAL LIFE?

**Fasting from actions that we do
simply to fill time:**
diversions; escapes.
Activity can be addictive.
Being constantly active tends to be aided and abetted
by contemporary culture with its fast pace,
its demands,
its attractions—
all of which
tend to work against
an inward turn.

Fasting from worry.
Be mindful of one's own worry tendencies.
Notice why and when and how they appear.
What does worry feel like?
What does it accomplish?
What seems to cause it?
Does it not stem from ego-centric concerns—
the very concerns spiritual teachers ask us to minimize or re-direct?

Jesus' advice:
Consider the lilies,
how they grow,
how they are provided for.

Consider the birds
who do not plant
and store crops
and yet find food.

Go outside.
Take a look!

Fasting from expectations for specific results.
Recognizing we cannot control
or own the outcome.
Being attached to expectations
often results in frustration and suffering.
"Do the work,
then let it go."
That is the advice of
ancient masters.
Not easy to do!

To let go of attachment to results,
even briefly,
requires a spiritual understanding
of ourselves and the world;
to recognize,
as many masters have said
what a small part we are
of an infinite,
interconnected
world.

What a privilege it is
to do our bit
however small.

Fasting from interactions,
at least temporarily,
in order that attention and energy can be directed inward.
Learning how not to be trapped in the roles we play
and the sense of self that these enforce.
It is especially important in Lenten times to refrain,
if one can,
from interactions that are energy draining
and function mainly as distractions,
or which tend to lock us into roles and expectations
that are too limiting or even harmful.

Fasting from unnecessary talk.
To be mindful.
To notice our speech patterns and tendencies.
To be aware of how speech,
which is essentially a communication tool,
is often used to obscure,
to cut off,
to not acknowledge and have genuine regard for the other.

To refrain from the kind of talk
that tends to pull us away from inner awareness;
from being present in the moment where we are.
And, of course,
to refrain from gossip and from speaking ill of other people;
to refrain from talk likely to cause harm
to others and/or one's self.

In times of inner change and growth.
one must take care,
to nurture and protect the tender green shoots of new growth.
That is why solitude and silence
are recommended spiritual practices.

Fasting from preferences:
Fasting from preconceived notions of how things are;
or how we think they should be.

Where *do* preferences come from?
What do they serve?
What problems can they cause?
Preferences are a mind-set we impose, or try to, on the world.
Preferences to a large event direct our actions.
Of course, preferences have a useful, practical purpose.
They steer us through complexities.
And preferences of a certain sort are essential to the spiritual life:
preferring truth to falsehood,
good to evil, for example.
But the spiritual problem with preferences is
that they tend to limit,
to shut down awareness
rather than letting it be open,
réceptive.
Preferences tend to keep us locked up within our own heads.
And when our preferences are thwarted,
frustration,
anger,
suffering results.
So what sorts of preferences are to be avoided?
Those which tend to be a deterrent to spiritual growth.

Meditation practices are useful
for recognizing and not getting hooked by preferences
as well as to discern which ones are spiritually useful.

Fasting from Judgment.
Jesus issued many warnings about judgment:
"Judge not that ye be not judged."
"Why do you see the speck in your neighbor's eye,
and fail to notice the log in your own?"

Judging, of the kind that is warned against by Jesus,
comes out of a presumption to know—
to know what is right and proper,
by which we usually mean
what we ourselves are doing.

An important Lenten practice is to work at becoming mindful
of when, and why we tend to make judgments
and with what result?
What purpose do our judgments seem to serve?
Are we trying to avoid or hide from our own insecurities?

And there is the question of *standards* of judgment.
The standards we use are usually a mixed bag of values
stemming from and/or serving our self-interest
even when we claim some higher validity for them,
such as the claim that our standards are God's.

The proper place for judgment in the spiritual life,
as Jesus and others remind, is in regard to oneself—
to judge as honesty as one can,
or dares to,
how far one is away from living the values
to which he/she aspires.

Fasting from ill-will that tends to lead to wrong doing.
Before wrong doing was a deed,
it was a thought.
It is important to recognize feelings of ill will as they arise,
and to become aware of their disadvantages.
Try to remember that it is the mind
that creates the reality with which we have to deal.
As Epictetus, a Stoic, put it:
it is not what happens
but our interpretation of what happens
that is the problem.
If we did not perceive the other as a threat,
or a situation as a problem,
we would be likely to deal with the person or event
in ways beneficial to ourselves
as well as them.

In Buddhist teachings
there are antidotes for dealing with negative mind states.
An antidote involves intentionally practicing a state of mind
opposite to the negative ones.
For example, in cases of envy or anger,
practice being patient.
Practice rejoicing in the success of others.
Practice being kind.
Practice recognizing how much others are like you—
wanting, fearing, avoiding, and seeking similar things.
All of this is not easy
but possible
and very beneficial.

A final word about fasting practices.
Though it is important to give up thoughts and practices
that are detrimental to spiritual growth,
it is also important to find out for oneself
what sort of effort is needed.
Too much effort often has the reverse effect
of attaching one more firmly to what needs to be given up.

Too little effort,
on the other hand,
keeps one from making needed life changes.
So, give up what you need to for spiritual growth
but do it gently,
if you can.
That is the advice the Taoists of ancient China gave.
Learn from nature…where nothing seems forced.
Balance effort with receptivity.
More on that in the **Almsgiving** section
that comes next.

ALMSGIVING:

How Giving and Receiving are Intertwined

The almsgiving practice of Lent
reverses the usual desiring trajectory—
a giving away rather than acquiring,
a letting go
rather than clinging to
possessions.

Almsgiving is a kind of *purification* process:
a way to lessen the tyranny of the "I"
and direct awareness and energy outward
toward the needs of others—
emotional
as well as material.

Almsgiving grows out of allegiance to a higher order of things;
out of a recognition of the interdependence of all living things.
Otherwise, the giving away that almsgiving is,
may not make sense.

Almsgiving is an attitude toward and about possessions.
What does it mean to possess…
or think one does?
And how can that be a spiritual problem?

Our attachments to possessions
can take many forms.
The most obvious of these are things we think we own:
the amount of money in our accounts,
the objects we've been given or bought.
None of these will last, of course,
but that does not seem to stop us
from trying to get as much as we can.

Not only are we attached
to what we think are our possessions;
attached to the wanting them,
attached to the getting them,
we worry about their being lost or stolen.
Possessions take up a lot of space
both inside our heads
as well as our rooms.

No material possession will be ours after we die.
So why *do* we cling to them?
Why do we want them so much?
One answer might be security, or the attempt at it.
Piling up what Jesus called "treasures on earth",
to try to keep at bay
a sometimes haunting sense of futility; of emptiness.
But it doesn't work, does it?
"More" never seems to be enough.
Are there, then,
other kinds of treasures
we should want?

Attachment to material things is a kind of bondage,
spiritual masters say.
Selfish attachment brings suffering;
Selfish attachment brings fear.

It is not the *thing* that is the problem
but our attachment to it—
so said the Buddha,
and the Stoics
and Jesus,
to name a few.

How can that situation be changed?
Not necessarily by rigorous efforts to overcome attachment.
That is more likely to strengthen it.
What *can* help is a gradual refocus of attention
a concern for what Jesus called the "things of heaven"—
that which can bring
the abiding satisfaction
that we want.

Money and the spiritual life.

There is, perhaps,
no clearer indication of one's spiritual condition
than ones attitude toward
and use of money.

Why is the desire for money,
the seeking of it,
so powerful?
What are the values,
the goals,
the objectives we have in mind?

Money is important
but various valuations of it are possible
from an overriding preoccupation (obsession)
to a kind of detachment,
aware of the limits
of what money can buy
and what it can't.

"He/she is richest," Jesus said,
"whose life is centered on that that which can never be possessed."

"Blessed are the poor in spirit, for theirs is the kingdom of heaven."

Lay up for yourselves "treasures in heaven",
in some realm
beyond loss and decay.

Almsgiving—fasting and prayer.
There is an intimate relation between
almsgiving
and the practices of fasting and of prayer.
Almsgiving is not simply giving money and material goods,
though there are many situations where that is called for,
but almsgiving is the open spirit in relationships, as well:
to give(be) what is needed.
To know what is actually needed,
what would be appropriate and timely,
is not something determined by us.
Rather, it is a response to a sense of the Spiritual work.
Being attentive to the Spirit
directs us to do what is needed.
This could be a listening ear,
an encouraging word,
a joke to lift a spirit,
or it could be knowing when
to leave the person
or situation
alone.

What does **the moment require?**

That is always the spiritual question.
Ancient Chinese philosophers advised doing the right thing,
at the right time,
for the right reason.

Thus, "Emptiness" (humility) is a factor in almsgiving;
to not presume the needs of others.

To bring to interactions
something of the awareness,
the receptivity,
of prayer.

To glimpse,
if only for a moment,
the sacred community
that all humans
share.

When Jesus gave instructions for giving alms,
his emphasis was that it needs to be done
"in secret".
"Beware." he said,
"of practicing your piety in a public way
in order to gain recognition.
"When you give alms,
do not let your left hand know what the right is doing."
(Mt. 6: 1, 3-4)

What is the problem with seeking recognition for good works?

Why
(and how)
does recognition seeking
tend to become
a spiritual trap?

Almsgiving needs to be done in secret
so that it is not bound by,
not attached to,
any sort of recognition even of and by oneself.
Almsgiving, then, simply flows naturally
from a heart of compassion.
It is effortless,
not premeditated.
It is simply the response of a trained heart
to human need.

There are numerous Asian insights about this kind of giving:
an analogy provided by the author of *Zen and the Art of Archery* is
that an action should be as effortless and timely
as snow falling off the branch of a tree
when the weather has warmed.
This takes much attentiveness
and much practice.

Taoism speaks of effortless action *(wu wei).*
Effortless action means that it is not "I" who does the action,
but the action is getting done through me.
"Thy will be done on earth, as it is in heaven",
is how Jesus put it.

Effortless action means cooperating with the forces of the universe
rather than imposing one's own will on a situation.
"The right action
at the right time
for the right reason."

What a lot of spiritual practice it takes to do this!

Is almsgiving giving or is it receiving?
The answer is: both.
What we are able to give
is something we have received.
The giving
arises out of
an awareness of the interconnectedness
of all living things,
and the various ways
we are linked
in community.

To receive in every act of giving
involves
(requires)
a sense of the Transcendent…
requires prayer
or at least, a *mindfulness*
that resembles it.

St. Francis said: "It is in giving that we receive,…"

Almsgiving
is not a diminishment of our resources
but an act
through which we receive
a richness
no money could buy.

Gratitude is a major component
of each of the Lenten practices.

Prayer:
a recognition of the gift
that is life
and all that sustains it.
Gratitude to the benevolent-seeming Source
of all that is.

Fasting
by refraining from what is not essential,
what is distracting;
fasting from selfish actions,
we become aware of
what is more important
than self-gratification.
We become aware and grateful for that which sustains
and deeply satisfies.

Almsgiving:
Giving arising out of gratitude for life
and all that sustains it.
We give
(and receive)
in gratitude for our ability and means
to provide some
of what others need.

Practice gratitude!
That's what it means
to give alms.

PRAYER:
Communion with the Divine

Prayer is, perhaps, *the* basic spiritual practice:
an openness to the "framing Mystery" of our lives;
an orientation toward Something
even if that something has no name
(though names can point toward it),
and even if one is not quite sure
there is "anyone" out there.
Even then
it can seem as if there is a distant pole
that exerts a powerful attraction;
that draws awareness
toward itself.

Prayer is sensing a Presence
of that which evades description.

Feeling "summoned";
Being "questioned".

Prayer is a kind of fasting—
fasting from our attempts
to impose our will on a situation;
to try to get our needs,
as we perceive them,
met—and as soon as possible.

A paradox of the spiritual life
is that in letting go
we find what we've been seeking.
even though
we may not know
its name.

Mindfulness,
discernment,
silence,
openness.

Ceasing from usual activity.

Opening minds and hearts
to that Great Mystery
that many call
"God."

Faith, it has been said,
is "the substance of things hoped for;
the evidence of things not seen".

Prayer is trusting in
what we can't quite know
but which seems
to lure us
toward it.

The reverent unknowing
that is prayer.

We do not presume
but learn
how to be silent—
how to wait.

"Be still…and know…"

Wait for the divine presence,
in whatever form
it may appear.

Jesus said:
"Whenever you pray....
go into your room
and shut the door
and pray to your Father who is in secret."
(Matthew 6:6)

What are the "doors"that must be closed for prayer?

Physical withdrawal is important,
but after that,
the difficult task of closing the inner doors,
the mind chatter
that keeps us thinking
planning
remembering.

Practice in being silent
is an essential component
of many spiritual traditions.

In silence,
we no longer cling to words.
We no longer cling to expectations.
Not even do we cling
to who we think we are.

Not clinging is silence.
There is nothing to grasp:
no foothold.
no handhold.
no mind hold.

Sit quietly.
Notice the breath.
Let thoughts and feelings arise.
Let thoughts and actions go.
Notice. Simply notice.

Do not expect results.
Do not expect special feelings.
Simply be present.
Be mindful of breath.

How are we linked to the world?
By the filaments of our own efforts?
By the web of our own talk?

What if there is a connection
deeper than the ones we make?

A Silence
more eloquent
than our profoundest speech?

In prayer,
we can come to know
that we are not
the sole originator
of what we do.

We participate in a vast
interconnected universe
out of which we've come,
and to which,
we are forever bound.

Prayer often begins in words
but as it deepens
words grow fewer.

Vaster are the spaces between the words.

Deeper the silence
that slowly takes
the place of words.

Deeper yet the silence
empty of all
but
the One
whose name is
hallowed.

In silence, we shrink down into ourselves.
We may feel helpless and fight letting go.
And yet
it can be this sense of lack
that opens us
toward prayer.

For the silence that is prayer
is not an absence;
it is not a loss.

The silence that is prayer
is the silence
of intimate communion.

Take time to sit.
Sit with the breath.
Sit in and toward
that benevolent Mystery
out of which we have come,
and to which
we are forever bound.

Postscript

**Learning from Jesus
how to pray.**

"Our Father, who art in heaven…"
We are parented
from a place beyond
any we can see.

"Hallowed be Thy Name"
Hallowed be
something at least…
some place,
some name
that lures us
toward it.

**"Thy Kingdom come,
Thy will be done,
on earth,
as it is in heaven."**
Enter the shelters
of our projects and our plans.
Carry us
beyond all these
into the vastness
of benevolence.

"Give us this day our daily bread."
Give us what we really need.
Help us to trust
so that we don't feel the need
to store.

**"Forgive us our trespasses
as we forgive…**
O Thou, who makes forgiveness possible,
Let not our resentments
close us off
from a love that is abundant.

"Deliver us from evil…"
Even if,
we have to
give up
being selfish.

For Thine *is* the Kingdom."
And the Lenten practices
are reminders.